LIGHTNING
BOLT
BOOKS™

It's Snowy Today

Kristin Sterling

Lerner Publications Company
Minneapolis

To my mom and dad, for making snowy days so fun

Lerner Publications Company
A division of Lerner Publishing Group, Inc.
241 First Avenue North
Minneapolis, MN 55401 U.S.A.

Website address: www.lernerbooks.com

Library of Congress Cataloging-in-Publication Data

Sterling, Kristin.
    It's Snowy Today / by Kristin Sterling.
        p.   cm. — (Lightning Bolt Books™—What's the Weather Like?)
    Includes index.
    ISBN 978-0-7613-4258-8 (lib. bdg. : alk. paper)
    1. Snow—Juvenile literature. 2. Winter—Juvenile literature. I. Title.
    QC926.37.S74 2010
    551.57'84—dc22   2008051584

Manufactured in the United States of America
1 2 3 4 5 6 — BP — 15 14 13 12 11 10

Contents

The Wonder of Snow

Snowflakes swoop and swirl to the ground through the frosty morning sky.

Earth is covered with
a pale white blanket.
It's a perfect snowy day!

Snowflakes are made of ice crystals. They form inside the clouds.

Snowflakes form when the temperature of clouds drops below the freezing point.

Each six-sided snowflake is a tiny work of art.

Have you seen one up close?

Snow falls gently some days in the winter. You can catch lacy flakes in your hands.

Snow falls hard and fast during blizzards. Cars get buried in giant snowdrifts.

A heavy coating of snow buries these cars after a blizzard.

Snowy Day Fun

There is so much you can do on snowy days! It's time to get dressed.

Put on your coat, hat, and boots. Remember your mittens too!

Winter clothes help kids stay warm when they play outside in the snow.

You can build fun forts in the snow. This fort is a great place to hide!

Wet, heavy snow works best for building forts.

You can make a friendly snowman. Mr. Chilly needs a scarf and hat!

13

Put on your ice skates and swirl around on a pond. Play hockey with friends.

Sled down steep hills with your family members.

Watch out for that tree!

When your
toes are
cold and
your nose
is red,
it's time
to head
inside!

16

Sip hot chocolate near a roaring fire. Warm your feet in thick, dry socks.

A roaring fire can warm your toes on a chilly winter day.

Winter Adaptations

People can warm up in houses in the winter. **What do wild animals do?**

Bears eat a lot in the summer and hibernate in the winter.

When bears hibernate, they go into a sleeplike state. This helps them survive cold weather.

Geese fly to warmer places.

Squirrels store away extra food in secret spots.

Many animals burrow under the snow or snuggle with others to stay warm.

This rabbit sits in a burrow it dug in the snow.

Trees lose their leaves in the autumn. Branches freeze in the winter.

Sometimes we hear a **CRACK!** A branch has broken under the weight of the snow.

Heavy snow makes tree branches droop.

Scientists study the weather using many kinds of tools.

These scientists are studying weather patterns on computer screens.

They can tell us if severe weather is on the way so we can stay safe.

TV weather reports can warn us if scientists expect a blizzard.

Another Snowy Day

Clouds clear away and the snowfall stops. Another snowy day has ended.

What will you do on the next snowy day?

The Snowflake Man

Wilson Bentley was born in 1865. He grew up in Vermont. As a child, he loved to catch snowflakes and study them. He noticed that they were unique, like people.

Wilson studied snow for the rest of his life. He discovered a way to take pictures of snowflakes before they melted. He wrote a book, *Snow Crystals*, which had more than two thousand pictures of snowflakes. Today Wilson is known as "Snowflake Bentley."

Fun Facts

- The snowiest large city in the United States is Rochester, New York.

- Snowflakes have many shapes. The shapes depend on what kind of clouds they come from.

- Snow is not white. It is clear. Snow appears white because it is reflecting light.

- Snow starts out as water vapor, which rises from Earth into the sky.

- You can create snowflakes by folding and cutting paper. Remember to make six sides!

Glossary

adaptation: a change that a living thing goes through so it fits in better with its environment

blizzard: a heavy snowstorm

burrow: to dig a hole for shelter. *Burrow* can also refer to the hole itself.

hibernate: to spend the winter in a sleeplike state

snowdrift: a bank of blown snow

snowflake: a crystal of snow

Further Reading

Brett, Jan. *The Mitten*. New York: Putnam, 1989.

Martin, Jacqueline Briggs. *Snowflake Bentley*. Boston: Houghton Mifflin, 1998.

Rylant, Cynthia. *Snow*. Orlando, FL: Harcourt, 2008.

Snowflake Bentley
http://www.snowflakebentley.com

Sterling, Kristin. *It's Cloudy Today*. Minneapolis: Lerner Publications Company, 2010.

Weather Wiz Kids
http://www.weatherwizkids.com

Index

Photo Acknowledgments

The images in this book are used with the permission of: © Tom Shaw/Getty Images, p. 1; © Ariel Skelley/Photographer's Choice/Getty Images, p. 2; © Adam Gryko/Dreamstime.com, p. 4; © Adie Bush/Cultura/Getty Images, p. 5; © Adalberto Rios Szalay/Sexto Sol/Getty Images, p. 6; NOAA's National Weather Service (NWS) Collection, pp. 7, 28; © Shawn and Sue Roberts/Dreamstime.com, p. 8; © Richard Goodrich/Dreamstime.com, p. 9; © Marta Johnson, p. 10; © Jose Luis Pelaez/Iconica/Getty Images, p. 11; © Vicky Kasala Productions/Photodisc/Getty Images, p. 12; © Paul Maguire/Dreamstime.com, p. 13; © LWA/Dann Tardiff/Blend Images/Getty Images, p. 14; © LWA/Photographer's Choice/Getty Images, p. 15; © Caroline Woodham/Photodisc/Getty Images, p. 16; © Monkey Business Images/Dreamstime.com, p. 17; © Photodisc/Getty Images, p. 18; © Stouffer Productions/Animals Animals, p. 19; © Randy Harris/Dreamstime.com, p. 20; © Mark Newman/Aflo Foto Agency/Photolibrary, p. 21; © Stubblefieldphoto/Dreamstime.com, p. 22; © Photononstop/SuperStock, p. 23; © Scientifica/Visuals Unlimited, Inc., p. 24; © Karolina Wolko, p. 25; © ULTRA.F/Digital Vision/Getty Images, p. 26; © Darren Baker/Dreamstime.com, p. 27; © Viviolsen/Dreamstime.com, p. 30; © Andrea Rugg Photography, p. 31.

Cover: © iStockphoto.com/Akaplummer.